# LADY

## OF THE

# MOON

# LADY

## OF THE

# MOON

Poems by
**Amy Lowell**
**Mary Meriam**

Essay by
**Lillian Faderman**

Headmistress Press

ISBN-13: 978-0692388518
ISBN-10: 0692388516

Versions of Lillian Faderman's essay, "'Which, Being Interpreted, Is as May Be, or Otherwise' Ada Dwyer Russell in Amy Lowell's Life and Work" have appeared in *Gay Books Bulletin* 1.2 (Summer 1979): 23-27; *Surpassing the Love of Men Romantic Friendship and Love Between Women from the Renaissance to the Present,* by Lillian Faderman (William Morrow, 1981); and *Amy Lowell: American Modern,* edited by Adrienne Munich and Melissa Bradshaw (Rutgers University Press, 2004). Used by permission of Lillian Faderman.

Poems by Amy Lowell are in the Public Domain.

Cover photograph of Ada Dwyer Russell used by permission, Utah State Historical Society, all rights reserved.

Cover and book design by Mary Meriam.

## P U B L I S H E R

Headmistress Press
60 Shipview Lane
Sequim, WA 98382
Telephone: 917-428-8312
Email: headmistresspress@gmail.com
Website: headmistresspress.blogspot.com

For Amy & Ada

# Contents

## I. Amy Lowell: Selected Poems

## II. Lillian Faderman: Essay

"Which, Being Interpreted, Is as May Be, or Otherwise"
Ada Dwyer Russell in Amy Lowell's Life and Work / 35

## III. Mary Meriam: Sonnet Sequence

# I. AMY LOWELL

## Vernal Equinox

The scent of hyacinths, like a pale mist, lies between me and my book;
And the South Wind, washing through the room,
Makes the candles quiver.
My nerves sting at a spatter of rain on the shutter,
And I am uneasy with the thrusting of green shoots
Outside, in the night.

Why are you not here to overpower me with your tense and urgent love?

# A Sprig of Rosemary

I cannot see your face.
When I think of you,
It is your hands which I see.
Your hands
Sewing,
Holding a book,
Resting for a moment on the sill of a window.
My eyes keep always the sight of your hands,
But my heart holds the sound of your voice,
And the soft brightness which is your soul.

## The Letter

Little cramped words scrawling all over the paper
Like draggled fly's legs,
What can you tell of the flaring moon
Through the oak leaves?
Or of my curtained window and the bare floor
Spattered with moonlight?
Your silly quirks and twists have nothing in them
Of blossoming hawthorns,
And this paper is dull, crisp, smooth, virgin of loveliness
Beneath my hand.

I am tired, Beloved, of chafing my heart against
The want of you;
Of squeezing it into little inkdrops,
And posting it.
And I scald alone, here, under the fire
Of the great moon.

## Strain

It is late
And the clock is striking thin hours,
But sleep has become a terror to me,
Lest I wake in the night
Bewildered,
And stretching out my arms to comfort myself with you,
Clasp instead the cold body of darkness.
All night it will hunger over me,
And push and undulate against me,
Breathing into my mouth
And passing long fingers through my drifting hair.
Only the dawn can loose me from it,
And the grey streaks of morning melt it from my side.

Bring many candles,
Though they stab my tired brain
And hurt it.
For I am afraid of the twining of the darkness
And dare not sleep.

## Prime

Your voice is like bells over roofs at dawn
When a bird flies
And the sky changes to a fresher color.

Speak, speak, Beloved.
Say little things
For my ears to catch
And run with them to my heart.

# The Garden by Moonlight

A black cat among roses,
Phlox, lilac-misted under a first-quarter moon,
The sweet smells of heliotrope and night-scented stock.
The garden is very still,
It is dazed with moonlight,
Contented with perfume,
Dreaming the opium dreams of its folded poppies.
Firefly lights open and vanish
High as the tip buds of the golden glow
Low as the sweet alyssum flowers at my feet.
Moon-shimmer on leaves and trellises,
Moon-spikes shafting through the snow ball bush.
Only the little faces of the ladies' delight are alert and staring,
Only the cat, padding between the roses,
Shakes a branch and breaks the chequered pattern
As water is broken by the falling of a leaf.
Then you come,
And you are quiet like the garden,
And white like the alyssum flowers,
And beautiful as the silent sparks of the fireflies.
Ah, Beloved, do you see those orange lilies?
They knew my mother,
But who belonging to me will they know
When I am gone?

## Venus Transiens

Tell me,
Was Venus more beautiful
Than you are,
When she topped
The crinkled waves,
Drifting shoreward
On her plaited shell?
Was Botticelli's vision
Fairer than mine;
And were the painted rosebuds
He tossed his lady
Of better worth
Than the words I blow about you
To cover your too great loveliness
As with a gauze
Of misted silver?

For me,
You stand poised
In the blue and buoyant air,
Cinctured by bright winds,
Treading the sunlight.
And the waves which precede you
Ripple and stir
The sands at my feet.

## Summer Rain

All night our room was outer-walled with rain.
Drops fell and flattened on the tin roof,
And rang like little disks of metal.
Ping!—Ping!—and there was not a pinpoint of silence between them.
The rain rattled and clashed,
And the slats of the shutters danced and glittered.
But to me the darkness was red-gold and crocus-coloured
With your brightness,
And the words you whispered to me
Sprang up and flamed—orange torches against the rain.
Torches against the wall of cool, silver rain!

# Madonna of the Evening Flowers

All day long I have been working,
Now I am tired.
I call: "Where are you?"
But there is only the oak-tree rustling in the wind.
The house is very quiet,
The sun shines in on your books,
On your scissors and thimble just put down,
But you are not there.
Suddenly I am lonely:
Where are you?
I go about searching.

Then I see you,
Standing under a spire of pale blue larkspur,
With a basket of roses on your arm.
You are cool, like silver,
And you smile.
I think the Canterbury bells are playing little tunes.

You tell me that the peonies need spraying,
That the columbines have overrun all bounds,
That the pyrus japonica should be cut back and rounded.
You tell me these things.
But I look at you, heart of silver,
White heart-flame of polished silver,
Burning beneath the blue steeples of the larkspur,
And I long to kneel instantly at your feet,
While all about us peal the loud sweet *Te Deums* of
        the Canterbury bells.

# July Midnight

Fireflies flicker in the tops of trees,
Flicker in the lower branches,
Skim along the ground.
Over the moon-white lilies
Is a flashing and ceasing of small, lemon-green stars.
As you lean against me,
Moon-white,
The air all about you
Is slit, and pricked, and pointed with sparkles of lemon-green flame
Starting out of a background of vague, blue trees.

## Wheat-In-The-Ear

You stand between the cedars and the green spruces,
Brilliantly naked
And I think:
    What are you,
    A gem under sunlight?
    A poised spear?
    A jade cup?
You flash in front of the cedars and the tall spruces,
And I see that you are fire—
Sacrificial fire on a jade altar,
Spear-tongue of white, ceremonial fire.
My eyes burn,
My hands are flames seeking you,
But you are as remote from me as a bright pointed planet
Set in the distance of an evening sky.

# The Weather-Cock Points South

I put your leaves aside,
One by one:
The stiff, broad outer leaves;
The smaller ones,
Pleasant to touch, veined with purple;
The glazed inner leaves.
One by one
I parted you from your leaves,
Until you stood up like a white flower
Swaying slightly in the evening wind.

White flower,
Flower of wax, of jade, of unstreaked agate;
Flower with surfaces of ice,
With shadows faintly crimson.
Where in all the garden is there such a flower?
The stars crowd through like lilac leaves
To look at you.
The low moon brightens you with silver.

The bud is more than the calyx.
There is nothing to equal a white bud,
Of no colour, and of all,
Burnished by moonlight,
Thrust upon by a softly-swinging wind.

## The Artist

Why do you subdue yourself in golds and purples?
Why do you dim yourself with folded silks?
Do you not see that I can buy brocades in any draper's shop,
And that I am choked in the twilight of all these colours.
How pale you would be, and startling,
How quiet;
But your curves would spring upward
Like a clear jet of flung water,
You would quiver like a shot-up spray of water,
You would waver, and relapse, and tremble.
And I too should tremble,
Watching.

Murex-dyes and tinsel—
And yet I think I could bear your beauty unshaded.

## The Taxi

When I go away from you
The world beats dead
Like a slackened drum.
I call out for you against the jutted stars
And shout into the ridges of the wind.
Streets coming fast,
One after the other,
Wedge you away from me,
And the lamps of the city prick my eyes
So that I can no longer see your face.
Why should I leave you,
To wound myself upon the sharp edges of the night?

## Left Behind

White phlox and white hydrangeas,
High, thin clouds,
A low, warm sun.
So it is this afternoon.
But the phlox will be a drift of petals,
And the hydrangeas stained and fallen
Before you come again.
I cannot look at the flowers,
Nor the lifting leaves of the trees.
Without you, there is no garden,
No bright colours,
No shining leaves.
There is only space,
Stretching endlessly forward –
And I walk, bent, unseeing,
Waiting to catch the first faint scuffle
Of withered leaves.

# Nerves

The lake is steel-coloured and umber,
And a clutter of gaunt clouds blows rapidly across the sky.

I wonder why you chose to be buried
In this little grave-yard by the lake-side.
It is all very well on blue mornings,
Summer mornings,
Autumn mornings polished with sunlight.
But in Winter, in the cold storms,
When there is no wind,
And the snow murmurs as it falls!
The grave-stones glimmer in the twilight
As though they were rubbed with phosphorous.
The direct road is up a hill,
Through woods—
I will take the lake road,
I can drive faster there.
You used to like to drive with me—
Why does death make you this fearful thing?
Flick!—flack!—my horse's feet strike the stones.
There is a house just round the bend.

# Grotesque

Why do the lilies goggle their tongues at me
When I pluck them;
And writhe, and twist,
And strangle themselves against my fingers,
So that I can hardly weave the garland
For your hair?
Why do they shriek your name
And spit at me
When I would cluster them?
Must I kill them
To make them lie still,
And send you a wreath of lolling corpses
To turn putrid and soft
On your forehead
While you dance?

## Bullion

My thoughts
Chink against my ribs
And roll about like silver hail-stones.
I should like to spill them out,
And pour them, all shining,
Over you.
But my heart is shut upon them
And holds them straitly.

Come, You! and open my heart;
That my thoughts torment me no longer,
But glitter in your hair.

# The Wheel of the Sun

I beg you
Hide your face from me.
Draw the tissue of your head-gear
Over your eyes.
For I am blinded by your beauty
And my heart is strained,
And aches,
Before you.

In the street,
You spread a brightness where you walk,
And I see your lifting silks
And rejoice;
But I cannot look up to your face.
You melt my strength,
And set my knees to trembling.

Shadow yourself that I may love you,
For now it is too great a pain.

# A Shower

The sputter of rain, flipping the hedgerows
And making the highways hiss,
How I love it!
And the touch of you upon my arm
As you press against me that my umbrella
May cover you.

Tinkle of drops on stretched silk
Wet murmur through green branches.

# April

A bird chirped at my window this morning,
And over the sky is drawn a light network of clouds.
Come,
Let us go out into the open,
For my heart leaps like a fish that is ready to spawn.

I will lie under the beech-trees,
Under the grey branches of the beech-trees,
In a blueness of little squills and crocuses.
I will lie among the little squills
And be delivered of this overcharge of beauty,
And that which is born shall be a joy to you
Who love me.

# In a Garden

Gushing from the mouths of stone men
To spread at ease under the sky
In granite-lipped basins,
Where iris dabble their feet
And rustle to a passing wind,
The water fills the garden with its rushing,
In the midst of the quiet of close-clipped lawns.

Damp smell the ferns in tunnels of stone,
Where trickle and plash the fountains,
Marble fountains, yellowed with much water.

Splashing down moss-tarnished steps
It falls, the water;
And the air is throbbing with it;
With its gurgling and running;
With its leaping, and deep, cool murmur.

And I wished for night and you.
I wanted to see you in the swimming-pool,
White and shining in the silver-flecked water.

While the moon rode over the garden,
High in the arch of night,
And the scent of the lilacs was heavy with stillness.

Night and the water, and you in your whiteness, bathing!

# Aubade

As I would free the white almond from the green husk
So would I strip your trappings off,
Beloved.
And fingering the smooth and polished kernel
I should see that in my hands glittered a gem beyond counting.

# Interlude

When I have baked white cakes
And grated green almonds to spread upon them;
When I have picked the green crowns from the strawberries
And piled them, cone-pointed, in a blue and yellow platter;
When I have smoothed the seam of the linen I have been working;
What then?
To-morrow it will be the same:
Cakes and strawberries,
And needles in and out of cloth.
If the sun is beautiful on bricks and pewter,
How much more beautiful is the moon,
Slanting down the gauffered branches of a plum-tree;
The moon,
Wavering across a bed of tulips;
The moon,
Still,
Upon your face.
You shine, Beloved,
You and the moon.
But which is the reflection?
The clock is striking eleven.
I think, when we have shut and barred the door,
The night will be dark
Outside.

# Paradox

You are an amethyst to me,
Beating dark slabs of purple
Against quiet smoothnesses of heliotrope,
Sending the wine-colour of torches
Rattling up against an avalanche of pale windy leaves.

You enter my heart as twilight
Seeping softly among the ghosts of beeches
In a glade where the last light cleaves for an instant
        upon the swung lash of a water fall.
You oversweep me with the splendid flashing of your darkness,
And my flowers are tinted with the light of your thin grey moon.
An amethyst garden you are to me,
And in your sands I write my poems,
And plant my heart for you in deathless yew trees
That their leaves may shield you from the falling snow.

Open your purple palaces for my entertainment,
Welcome my feet upon your polished floors,
And keep in your brazier always
One red hot coal;
For I come at the times which suit me,
Morning or evening,
And I am cold when I come down the long alleys to you.
Clang the doors against the multitude who would follow me.
Is not this my chamber where I would sleep?

# A Rainy Night

Shadows,
And white, moving light,
And the snap and sparkle of rain on the window,
An electric lamp in the street
Is swinging, tossing,
Making the rain-runnelled window-glass
Glitter and palpitate.
In its silver lustre
I can see the old four-post bed,
With the fringes and balls of its canopy.
You are lying beside me, waiting,
But I do not turn,
I am counting the folds of the canopy.
You are lying beside me, waiting,
But I do not turn.
In the silver light you would be too beautiful,
And there are ten pleats on this side of the bed canopy,
And ten on the other.

## A Decade

When you came, you were like red wine and honey,
And the taste of you burnt my mouth with its sweetness.
Now you are like morning bread,
Smooth and pleasant.
I hardly taste you at all for I know your savour,
But I am completely nourished.

# Penumbra

As I sit here in the quiet Summer night,
Suddenly, from the distant road, there comes
The grind and rush of an electric car.
And, from still farther off,
An engine puffs sharply,
Followed by the drawn-out shunting scrape of a freight train.
These are the sounds that men make
In the long business of living.
They will always make such sounds,
Years after I am dead and cannot hear them.

Sitting here in the Summer night,
I think of my death.
What will it be like for you then?
You will see my chair
With its bright chintz covering
Standing in the afternoon sunshine,
As now.
You will see my narrow table
At which I have written so many hours.
My dogs will push their noses into your hand,
And ask—ask—
Clinging to you with puzzled eyes.

The old house will still be here,
The old house which has known me since the beginning.
The walls which have watched me while I played:
Soldiers, marbles, paper-dolls,
Which have protected me and my books.

The front-door will gaze down among the old trees
Where, as a child, I hunted ghosts and Indians;
It will look out on the wide gravel sweep
Where I rolled my hoop,
And at the rhododendron bushes
Where I caught black-spotted butterflies.

The old house will guard you,
As I have done.
Its walls and rooms will hold you,
And I shall whisper my thoughts and fancies
As always,
From the pages of my books.

You will sit here, some quiet Summer night,
Listening to the puffing trains,
But you will not be lonely,
For these things are a part of me.
And my love will go on speaking to you
Through the chairs, and the tables, and the pictures,
As it does now through my voice,
And the quick, necessary touch of my hand.

# Frimaire

Dearest, we are like two flowers
Blooming last in a yellowing garden,
A purple aster flower and a red one
Standing alone in a withered desolation.

The garden plants are shattered and seeded,
One brittle leaf scrapes against another,
Fiddling echoes of a rush of petals.
Now only you and I nodding together.

Many were with us; they have all faded.
Only we are purple and crimson,
Only we in the dew-clear mornings,
Smarten into colour as the sun rises.

When I scarcely see you in the flat moonlight,
And later when my cold roots tighten,
I am anxious for morning,
I cannot rest in fear of what may happen.

You or I—and I am a coward.
Surely frost should take the crimson.
Purple is a finer color,
Very splendid in isolation.

So we nod above the broken
Stems of flowers almost rotted.
Many mornings there cannot be now
For us both. Ah, Dear, I love you!

# II. Lillian Faderman

AMY LOWELL first met Ada Dwyer Russell, an actress, in 1909, when Russell appeared in Boston in *The Dawn of a Tomorrow.* Three years later Russell returned to Boston to play the character lead in *The Deep Purple,* and their intimate relationship ostensibly began. Russell, at forty-nine Lowell's senior by eleven years, was charming, cultured, poised, intelligent, and feminine—in short, everything Lowell sought in a muse, a lover, and, as she expressed it in "A Fairy Tale" (1912), a travel companion "along the parching highroad of the world." She invited Russell to spend the summer of 1912 on her country estate in New Hampshire and then to accompany her to England where Lowell, who had recently discovered the imagist movement, planned to meet with Ezra Pound. Russell did not go to England because she was committed to a road company tour, but she did spend the following summer with Lowell, again on Lowell's country estate. As S. Foster Damon, a personal friend of the couple's and Lowell's first biographer, suggests, it was then that Lowell proposed a permanent relationship. Russell refused for the short term and continued touring but promised to reconsider Lowell's proposal once the tour was over. Clearly, Lowell had difficulty bridling her impatience. At one point, in February of 1914, she sought Russell out when the actress was playing in Chicago and again proposed that she give up the stage and come live with her.[1]

What passed between them cannot be determined with absolute certainty since Lowell asked that their letters to each other be destroyed upon her death, but it is possible to conjecture Lowell's emotional state during these years from the apparently autobiographical poems of her second volume, *Sword Blades and Poppy Seed* (1914). The poem "Patience," for example, appears to answer Russell's plea for more time. Lowell's response is that Russell is so perfect, so much what the poet needs, that she cannot help her impatience. As in many of her love poems to Russell, she represses what Margaret Anderson described as her "Roman emperor" persona,[2] presenting herself as imploring, apologetic, and entirely at the mercy of the beloved who, in a series of images, is depicted as goddess, mother, healer, and holder of the sole and elemental power to rescue the speaker from alienation and pain:

Be patient with you?
   You! My sun and moon!
My basketful of flowers!
My money-bag of shining dreams! My hours,
   Windless and still, of afternoon!
You are my world and I your citizen.
   What meaning can have patience then?[3]

Other poems of this volume continue Lowell's suppliant lover's tone. In "Apology," a poem in which she employs the imagery of chivalry, Lowell is a young knight who is ecstatic that (s)he has been granted her beloved's favors, but (s)he has been sworn to silence:

You blazon me with jewelled insignia
. . .   And yet
        You set
The word upon me, unconfessed
        To go unguessed.

The poem itself is, of course, an instance of her loving disobedience. Not only does she admit here that she has been shouting the secret of her good fortune everywhere, but the poem publishes the secret for posterity to see:

Be not angry with me that I bear
    Your colours everywhere,
    All through each crowded street,
        And meet
The wonder-light in every eye,
        As I go by.

The "Apology" of the title is therefore wittily undercut by her demonstration that she glories in divulging their secret—though by omitting gender reference and relying on what has been a universal assumption of heterosexuality in love poetry she does keep its lesbian content closeted. (Readers who wish to be unaware of it can permit themselves to be charmed by the role reversal: a female knight addressing a presumably male beloved.)

Lowell's uncertainties in the course of her

courtship are revealed in this volume as well. "The Taxi,"
for example, expresses confusion and anger at the
separations from Russell that are imposed on her:

When I go away from you
The world beats dead
Like a slackened drum.
I call out for you against the jutted stars
And shout into the ridges of the wind.
Streets coming fast,
One after the other,
Wedge you away from me,
And the lamps of the city prick my eyes
So that I can no longer see your face.
Why should I leave you,
To wound myself upon the sharp edges of the night?

But this demanding tone is rare in these courtship poems,
even those that hint at Lowell's unhappy struggle as she
sought commitment from Russell before the actress was
ready to give it. Typically, Lowell is apologetic, turning
her anger inward, criticizing herself for her impatience. In
"A Blockhead" she is furious with her own "too hasty
hand," which she holds responsible for threatening that
which had brought her joy. Perhaps Russell delivered an
ultimatum at this point, insisting that Lowell cease
pressuring her or risk losing her. The same self-
castigation is reflected in her short poem, "A Bungler":

You glow in my heart
Like the flames of uncounted candles.

But when I go to warm my hands,
My clumsiness overturns the light,
And then I stumble
Against the tables and chairs.

In "Stupidity" Lowell depicts herself as a lover who
bruised her beloved's fragile rose by her "clumsy touch,"
and she chides herself, swearing she is even more grieved
by her action than the beloved.

In May 1914, Russell accepted another invitation
to accompany Lowell to Europe, and there the two
agreed to a trial arrangement upon their return: for six
months Russell would share Lowell's home, Sevenels, in a
business arrangement, assisting the poet with her literary
pursuits and receiving for her work the same sum she
would have earned had she continued on stage during
those months.[4] The great success of the trial period is
attested to by the fact that Russell remained to trudge
"the parching highroad of the world" (albeit in grand
style) with Lowell until Lowell's death eleven years later.
She became not only Lowell's muse and lover, but also, as
the nickname that Lowell coined for her suggests, her
rock: Ada was Pete, Peter, or Mrs. Peter (the latter
perhaps in deference to her essential femininity).
Elizabeth Sergeant, an intimate of the two, observed in
1927, shortly after Lowell's death, that the poet had
accomplished ten times more in the last decade and a half
of her life than most do in a half century.[5] Sergeant was
surely aware that the preponderance of Lowell's vast

accomplishments dated from 1912, the year Russell came into her life. Lowell's literary output during those years include nine books of poetry, four books of prose, the editing of five anthologies, and numerous appearances all over the country as a popular reader of her own work. And, as Lowell acknowledged, it was Russell who made that prodigious output possible, not only in her roles of mate and muse but also in her vast variety of other functions: overseer of the estate, wifely presider over Lowell's table and cocktail parties, virtual bodyguard, governess to Lowell's ill-mannered youth persona, literary assistant, and consultant. Russell critiqued Lowell's poems, read page proofs, supervised her secretaries, soothed her ruffled feathers over bad reviews or literary disputes, soothed the ruffled feathers of others when Lowell had been too brusque with them, got rid of intrusive guests, and even coached Lowell in preparation of the dramatic monologues she read in public and on which so much of her reputation was (unfortunately) based. Russell was as lovingly solicitous of Lowell's welfare and as much a cheerleader of her success as Alice B. Toklas was of Gertrude Stein's.

Lowell admitted that she "owed everything to Ada," and she even suggested, only half-jokingly, that they erect a sign above the doorway at Sevenels: "Lowell and Russell, Makers of Fine Poems."[6] In lieu of that charming but perhaps too-telling gesture, Lowell hoped at least to dedicate her books to Russell, who forbade that tribute, finally relenting only with the last book Lowell saw to publication, her biography of John Keats. It may be that Russell gave permission for this dedication because, unlike most of Lowell's books, the Keats biography contained no love poetry to her and therefore could not have identified her to the public as the lesbian beloved and muse. But Lowell, like the knight in her poem "Apology" who cannot keep herself from boasting of her good fortune despite her promise to her beloved to maintain their secret, dedicated her Keats biography, "To A.D.R., This, and all my books. A.L."

The effect of Russell's presence on Lowell is the subject of numerous poems, some that were published during the poet's life; others—which may have been considered too revealing to be published while Lowell lived—were included in *Ballads for Sale* (1927), a posthumous volume edited by Russell two years after Lowell's death. These poems often reflect Lowell's view of their domestic bliss. In "Thorn Piece," for example, Lowell talks about the world being dark, but her beloved, who is gendered here by her bright dress, carries a lantern. The autobiographical details in the poem make it clear that the ungendered speaker is Lowell, who thanks Russell for having given her "fire, / And love to comfort, and speech to bind, / And the common things of morning and evening." In another poem from Ballads for Sale, "On Christmas Eve," she again thanks the beloved other woman for having

Lifted my eyes and made me whole,
And given me purpose, and held me faced
Toward the horizon you once had placed
As my aim's grand measure."

Another poem, "A Decade," which reflects on their years together, concludes, "I am completely nourished."

The greatest conflict in their relationship seems to have stemmed from Lowell's jealousy of Russell's visits to her daughter, who married soon after Russell came to live with Lowell. Lowell seems to have finally solved the problem of her beloved's periodic "desertions" by convincing her to invite her daughter and son-in-law (and later, grandchild) to Sevenels for their vacations and ultimately making them her family, too.

With Russell presiding over Lowell's table and her drawing room the couple became this continent's counterpart of Gertrude Stein and Alice B. Toklas in the social realm as well as the personal. Their friends, who were lured not only by Lowell's force and power but also by Russell's graciousness and charm, included many of the leading Anglo-American literary lights: Conrad Aiken, Robert Frost, D.H. Lawrence, Compton Mackenzie, Archibald MacLeish, Sara Teasdale, Louis Untermeyer, Elinor Wylie, and of course, numerous lesbian couples, including Margaret Anderson and Jane Heap, and Bryher and H.D.

It is interesting to note that many of their

heterosexual friends were in fact homophobic (or, more specifically, "lesbophobic"), but like Ernest Hemingway in his relationship with Stein and Toklas, they made an "exception" for Lowell and Russell. Lawrence's loving correspondence with Lowell, in which he ended every letter by sending his and Frieda's love to both Amy and Ada, did not prevent him from writing his lesbian-hating novella *The Fox;* nor did Compton Mackenzie refrain from penning his lesbian satire *Extraordinary Women* despite his fondness for Lowell and Russell and the fact that Lowell came to his defense when one of his novels was censored in Boston. Perhaps they knew and did not know at the same time that Lowell and Russell were a lesbian couple. The era seems to have encouraged such willful denial, but that denial also made possible, in an era when censorship was rife in American literature, the publication of some of the most remarkable, barely encoded, lesbian poems since Sappho.

## WARDING OFF THE "WATCH AND WARD SOCIETY"

As a mover and shaker in the literary world, a position she merited by virtue of both her social status and her popular success as a writer, Amy Lowell pioneered in the battle against censorship. She fought the Comstock Society's efforts to suppress Theodore Dreiser's novel *The Genius,* and she opposed the Boston banning of works by Compton Mackenzie and D.H.

Lawrence. She claimed to believe, as she wrote H.L. Mencken in support of his battle against censorship, "No country can hope to develop itself, unless its authors are permitted to educate it."[7]

But despite her expressed opposition to literary censorship, Lowell prided herself on being a pragmatist. In a 1915 letter to Richard Aldington she warned the novelist about the power and influence of the "Watch and Ward Society" and the necessity of eschewing in writing what it would find objectionable.[8] In 1918 she wrote D.H. Lawrence about his refusal to be practical about such matters. His novel *The Rainbow* had been suppressed because of two erotic passages—a heterosexual love scene between Ursula and Anton, and a lesbian scene between Ursula and Winifred. Lowell admonished,

I know there is no use in counselling you to make any concessions to public opinions in your books and, although I regret sincerely that you cut yourself off from being published by an outspokenness which the English public does not understand, I regret it not in itself . . . but simply because it keeps the world from knowing what a great novelist you are. I think that you could top them all if you would be a little more reticent on this one subject [of sex]. You need not change your attitude a particle, you can simply use the india rubber [eraser] in certain places, and then you can come into your own as it ought to be. . . When one is surrounded by prejudice and blindness, it seems to me that the only thing to do is to get over in spite of it and not constantly run foul of these same prejudices which, after all, hurts oneself and the spreading of one's work, and does not do a thing to right the prejudice.[9]

Needless to say, Lawrence did not take her advice seriously, but much of Lowell's own writing was predicated on such a view. With regard to lesbian subject matter in her poetry, she did not "change [her] attitude a particle," but she did "use an india rubber in certain places," though only perfunctorily, rubbing out of much of her love poetry only explicit references that would identify the gender of the speaker. She depended on the probability that her general public would read her love lyrics like her dramatic monologues—that is, assuming that the speaker was a (male) persona—and on the readers' habit of taking for granted heterosexuality in the absence of specific evidence to the contrary.

But her use of the "india rubber" was not more than perfunctory. Unlike in her monologues, in her lyric poems the speaker is not characterized into a dramatis persona, and Lowell often furnishes abundant autobiographical facts (e.g., descriptions of her estate, her sheepdogs, her illustrious family name) that make it quite clear to one who knows the details of her life that the speaker and the author of these poems are not disparate. She thus provides a double discourse, revealing herself sufficiently to those who might welcome the revelation while avoiding what would get her into trouble. In this way, Lowell warded off the "Watch and Ward Society" though she produced the most explicit (as well as eloquent and elegant) lesbian love poetry to have been written between the time of Sappho and the 1970s. She thumbed her nose at the forces that would repress her while appearing to have no intention of violating their strictures.

If we can believe the confessions she makes about the way she worked as a writer in her poem "To a Gentleman Who Wanted to See the First Drafts of My Poems in the Interests of Psychological Research into the Workings of the Creative Mind" (1927) Lowell may have revealed even the speaker's gender and more autobiographical references in the early drafts of her love poetry. "To a Gentleman" is based on an actual incident: a professor at the Carnegie Institute of Psychology wanted to analyze, he said, her creative processes. Lowell suspected, as she says in this poem, that he wanted to see when she was using a persona and when she was speaking for herself: "What is I, and what that other? That's your quest." And she refused him access to her early drafts and any other revelations, hinting that only Russell was privy to such secret information: "If I did consent, to please you, I should tell you packs of lies / To one only will I tell it, do I tell it all day long. / Only one can see the patches I work into quilts of song." (Lest we feel guilty for our present dissections, she exonerates us: "Still I have a word, one moment, stop, before you leave this room. / Though I shudder thinking of you wandering through my beds of bloom, / You may come with spade and shovel when I'm safely in the tomb.")

Yet Lowell's quite perfunctory encoding of lesbian subject matter was usually successful in throwing critics off the track, even after she was safely in her tomb. With few exceptions, commentators on her work appear to have believed that her poems of passion were literary exercises and that she revealed herself only in her poems of frustration. A notable exception is the hateful Clement Wood biography *Amy Lowell* (1926), in which he argued the year after she was placed "safely in the tomb" that her work was not "universal" because her love lyrics may "qualify [her] as an impassioned singer of her own desires; and she may well be a laureate of as many as stand beside her [i.e., other lesbians], [but] they do not word a common cry of many hearts."[10]

However, ironically, most critics who bludgeoned her work with an argumentum ad femina in the years after her death usually devalued it not because her passions were lesbian, but because she was an "old maid" who supposedly had no passions at all of her own. They observed that Lowell was overweight and unmarried and therefore, as one critic opined in the *Saturday Review of Literature* in 1927, her work is a "knell of personal frustration...an effort to hide the bare walls of the empty chambers of her heart."[11] Thirty years later, another critic wrote that Lowell confessed her lifelong sexual frustration in the opening lines of her monologue "Appuldurcombe Park" (1919): "I am a woman, sick for passion."[12] Until Jean Gould's 1975 biography, the first book to deal openly with Lowell's lesbian relationships, such outrageous misreading of the poet and her work had been unchallenged—and even subsequent studies, such as Richard Benvenuto's 1985 biography, ignore the significance of her lesbian relationship with Russell. (Benvenuto suggests, for example, that Lowell's poetry expresses "loneliness and longings which she, a fat woman, knew keenly."[13])

Indeed, hundreds of Lowell poems contradict such a reading. Even dramatic monologues and long poems such as "Appuldurcombe Park," "Pickthorne Manor" (1916), and "The Cremona Violin" (1916) may be seen not as expressing the author's personal frustration but rather as a demonstration of her interest in, and experience with, passions that society considered "illicit." Though these poems are about heterosexuals, they provide some commentary on homosexuality inasmuch as they have their source in Lowell's "outlaw" lesbian sensibility. Lowell even teases the reader on this point at times, as with the wittily titled, "Which, Being Interpreted, Is as May Be, Or Otherwise," a poem that is ostensibly about a man's illicit lust for a phantasmic married female.

But far more interesting, from the perspective of lesbian reading, are Lowell's many lyric poems that do not rely on the metaphor provided by illicit heterosexuality, as her dramatic poems do, but deal more directly with her passionate interest in another woman. In her numerous long monologue poems, she created always ostensibly heterosexual personae. Unlike her dramatic poems, her lesbian poems are invariably quite short, perhaps because short lyrics excuse the poet from presenting a characterized persona. Her selection of the length of her lesbian poems may indeed have been another means to enable her to encode her forbidden subject matter, to apply the india rubber, to ward off the "Watch and Ward Society."

## AMY LOWELL AS A POET OF EROS

Amy Lowell's lesbian love poems are often fresh, vivid, powerful, and (unlike many of her long poems, such as the famous "Patterns" (1916), with its clichéd heterosexual fantasy scene of a pink and silver female surrendering her soft and willing body to a heavy-booted man in a dashing uniform) they reflect their source in felt emotion. The lesbian poems in *Sword Blades and Poppy Seed* (1914), *Pictures of the Floating World* (1919), *What's O'Clock* (1925), and *Ballads for Sale* (1927), comprise one of the most detailed records in literature of an emotional and erotic relationship between two women, from their sometimes ecstatic, sometimes painful courtship; through the highs and lows of the life they built together; to

Lowell's anticipation of its end by her premature death.

Although Lowell admitted in correspondence to friends such as John Livingston Lowes that Russell was the subject of her love poetry, many critics have continued to have difficulty acknowledging that Lowell had a real-life source for the impassioned eroticism in her poems, that it was based on feelings she actually experienced.[14] In his 1975 study of Lowell, Glenn Richard Ruihley articulates what may be a major reason for their bafflement: Russell was "past middle age" when Lowell met her, he says, and "not graced with loveliness of face and form." Russell was, in fact, forty-nine when their relationship began, and she was quite beautiful if one's standard does not run to Hollywood starlet types. Ruihley, however, concludes that what Lowell must have loved in Russell was merely her "spiritual beauty," and he asserts that the relationship was therefore "removed...to a rare and platonic plane."[15] Under such assumptions one could easily miss the sexual meaning of many of the Ada poems.

Despite her vague attempts at disguise and the heterosexually biased critical obtuseness she could have counted on, Lowell may have felt that some of her lesbian poems were indeed too revealing for publication during her life, though after her death Russell published them in *Ballads for Sale*. Several such poems in the volume, including "Thorn Piece," "On Christmas Eve," "Hippocrene," and "Grievance," offer glimpses into the

Lowell-Russell household. Other poems in the volume are astonishingly explicit in their sexual meaning. "Paradox," for example, establishes Russell as the beloved through images that have come to stand for Russell in the body of Lowell's poetry. Here, as in many of the lesbian poems, Russell is associated with amethyst and purple, torches and snow, gardens and moonlight. The opening image, "You are an amethyst to me, / Beating dark slabs of purple," hints at an eroticism that becomes more insistent and even peremptory as the poem progresses:

Open your purple palaces for my entertainment,
Welcome my feet upon your polished floors,
And keep in your brazier always
One red hot coal;
For I come at the times which suit me,
Morning or evening,
And I am cold when I come down the long alleys to you.
Clang the doors against the multitude who would
        follow me.
Is not this my chamber where I would sleep?

The speaker's baronial tone as she addresses her beloved is offset and undercut by one of the several paradoxes of the poem—the other woman's subjugation of her: "You oversweep me with the splendid flashing of your darkness."

Lowell's stated position on sexual subject matter in literature was perhaps as disingenuous as that of Gertrude Stein's, who warned the young Ernest

Hemingway, much as Lowell warned D.H. Lawrence, that his story, "Up in Michigan," contained too much sexual detail, which made it impractical: it was *inaccroachable,* like a painting with salacious subject matter, which one could never exhibit. "There is no point" in such a work, Stein famously told Hemingway;[16] yet she herself wrote detailed, though encoded, descriptions of lesbian sex and even orgasm in works such as "As a Wife Has a Cow: A Love Story." And so did Lowell: One five-line poem from *Sword Blades and Poppy Seed,* for example, presents bold clitoral imagery that suggests lesbian sex:

As I would free the white almond from the green husk
So would I strip your trappings off,
Beloved.
And fingering the smooth and polished kernel
I should see that in my hands glittered a gem beyond
        counting.

Although the poem could be interpreted otherwise, Lowell hints at her intention to give the sexual meaning primacy by titling it "Aubade"—a dawn piece in which, traditionally, the poet thanks the beloved with whom he has spent the night for her sexual favors. "A Rainy Night" is explicit about the speaker's erotic tension in the moments that precede their lovemaking and about her trick for prolonging the delicious excitement of anticipation. Lowell sets the scene in a bedroom she shares with her beloved, which is illuminated only by an electric lamp in the street:

In its silver lustre
I can see the old four-post bed,
With the fringes and balls of its canopy.
You are lying beside me, waiting,
But I do not turn,
I am counting the folds of the canopy.
You are lying beside me, waiting,
But I do not turn.
In the silver light you would be too beautiful,
And there are ten pleats on this side of the bed canopy,
And ten on the other.

Other poems by Lowell may be read as lesbian primarily by virtue of their perspective: the gaze revealed in these poems is erotic and focused exclusively on a female, such as "In a Garden" (1914) in which the first-person speaker fantasizes that she could see her beloved "White and shining in the silver-flecked water / While the moon rode over the garden,... / Night and the water, and you in your whiteness, bathing!"

"On a Certain Critic," the concluding poem of *Pictures of the Floating World,* teases the reader into believing the literality of such poems by revealing Lowell's humorous disdain for those who confuse the poet's real lust with metaphor. In this poem John Keats (Lowell's alter ego) climbs Box Hill and there makes love to the Lady of the Moon (Lowell's frequent name for Russell). Keats and the Lady of the Moon are so close that he confuses his tears for hers. She is absolutely real to him.

Lowell then depicts the poet going home and writing a poem in memory of the experience. But in years to come, Lowell says, a "sprig" little gentleman will "turn over your manuscript with his mincing fingers." He will tabulate places and dates and conclude that Keats could not possibly have lain with Mistress Moon, that she was only "a copy-book maxim." The critic will then pontificate "about the spirit of solitude, / And the salvation of genius through the social order." Lowell wishes that Keats would be there to damn the critic's density with oaths. And she concludes the poem with a slap at Keats's critic and very possibly at her own critics as well:

But just snap your fingers,
You and the moon will still love,
When he and his papers have slithered away
In the bodies of innumerable worms.

## Two Speak Together

Lowell's most sustained effort at writing lesbian poetry resulted in a forty-three-poem sequence published under the heading "Two Speak Together" in her best-selling 1919 collection, *Pictures of the Floating World*. Judging from internal evidence such as changing and recurring season references, the poems seem to have been written over a four-year period, beginning not long after Lowell and Russell began living together. "A Decade," a poem in which she seems to celebrate their ten-year relationship, is confusing until it is remembered that Lowell first set eyes on Russell in 1909.

The autobiographical content of these poems is seldom disguised. Lowell admitted to friends that Russell was her inspiration, her "Madonna of the Evening Flowers," as one of the poems in this series is entitled;[17] and the poems are rife with references—to Sevenels and its lavish gardens, her animals, her habits such as writing while the rest of the household sleeps—that identify Lowell as the speaker. In "Preparation" a shopkeeper addresses the speaker as "Sir," but this attempt at "drag" is barely perfunctory and the speaker is often revealed to be a woman. For example, in "The Garden by Moonlight" the speaker thinks back through her mother in reflecting on her childless state (and it is impossible not to believe this is Amy Lowell in the garden of Sevenels):

Ah, Beloved, do you see those orange lilies?
They knew my mother,
But who belonging to me will they know
When I am gone?

In other poems as well, the speaker's gender is identified as female. Sometimes Lowell employs the metaphor of childbirth to describe her literary creations: in "April" she tells her beloved that her happiness with their life together will overflow into poetry:

I will lie among the little squills

And be delivered of this overcharge of beauty,
And that which is born shall be a joy to you
Who love me.

In "Interlude" she uses the metaphor of traditional
female tasks to describe her creation of imagist poems:
she is baking cakes and "smoothing the seam of the linen
I have been working." Obviously Lowell does not try
overly hard to disguise the speaker's gender in this poem,
despite the fact that her beloved here is specifically
associated with the moon, which is an Ada image in
"Two Speak Together" and throughout the Lowell canon.

There is little question that the speaker in all these
poems is female, and there is no question whatsoever that
the beloved is also female. In several of the poems the
beloved is compared to other women of great virtue or
beauty such as the Madonna or Venus (and Lowell's role
of poet becomes analogous to those of the early modern
artists who painted them). In others, Russell is depicted in
seductively feminine dress, as in "The Wheel of the Sun":
"I see your lifting silks and rejoice." Russell's pastimes are
also invariably feminine. In "A Sprig of Rosemary," for
example, she sews. In many of the poems she is described
in passively feminine terms, protected or made love to by
the speaker.

The forty-three poems in "Two Speak Together"
tell the story of Lowell and Russell in their first years as a
couple. As a poetic sequence that reveals a lesbian

relationship to any reader who would care to understand it, "Two Speak Together" was unprecedented in literature and had no equal until Adrienne Rich's sequence, "Twenty-one Love Poems," which was published in 1976. In "Two Speak Together" Lowell reflects the complexity of this relationship; their dyad nourishes Lowell, inspires her work, and arouses her passion, but it also creates great anxieties in her. Her loneliness when Russell leaves her periodically—usually to visit her daughter—is depicted as maddening. In the opening poems, "Vernal Equinox" and "The Letter," which concern the first year, Lowell already finds Russell's brief absence unbearable. Her missing of Russell has clear erotic overtones. In "Vernal Equinox" she demands to know, "Why are you not here to overpower me with your tense and urgent love?" In "The Letter" she laments, employing tropes that will be central to the sequence, "I scald alone, here, under the fire / Of the great moon."

In the next twenty poems of "Two Speak Together" Lowell is happier and fulfilled. She celebrates Russell's beauty in some of her very best work, including "Venus Transiens," in which Lowell compares herself trying to capture Russell on paper with Botticelli's attempt to capture Venus on canvas. Another poem in this sequence, "Madonna of the Evening Flowers" has been, after the far inferior "Patterns," the Lowell poem most likely to be anthologized, though its lesbian source is seldom discussed. It is a seminal poem in which Lowell, who was by no means conventionally pious, introduces the religious metaphors that were to become prevalent in many of her Ada Russell poems:

All day long I have been working,
Now I am tired.
I call: "Where are you?"
But there is only the oak-tree rustling in the wind.
The house is very quiet,
The sun shines in on your books,
On your scissors and thimble just put down,
But you are not there.
Suddenly I am lonely:
Where are you?
I go about searching.

Then I see you,
Standing under a spire of pale blue larkspur,
With a basket of roses on your arm.
You are cool, like silver,
And you smile.
I think the Canterbury bells are playing little tunes.

You tell me that the peonies need spraying,
That the columbines have overrun all bounds,
That the pyrus japonica should be cut back and rounded.
You tell me these things.
But I look at you, heart of silver,
White heart-flame of polished silver,
Burning beneath the blue steeples of the larkspur,
And I long to kneel instantly at your feet,
While all about us peal the loud sweet *Te Deums*
        of the Canterbury bells.

Many of the love poems in the final volume of

poetry Lowell prepared before her death, *What's O' Clock,*
draw on the religious metaphor that she established in
"Madonna of the Evening Flowers." She manages, in the
best Jacobean tradition, to combine metaphors of
religious worship with the metaphors of Eros, but unlike
those early poets, in her poems Eros is central. In "In
Excelsis," for example, Russell is the Eucharist, Christ,
and the beloved of the Songs of Solomon, but she is
especially the beautiful woman the speaker longs to
devour sexually as well as to worship:

As the perfume of jonquils, you come forth in the morning.
Young horses are not more sudden than your thoughts,
Your words are bees about a pear-tree ...
I drink your lips,
I eat the whiteness of your hands and feet.
My mouth is open,
As a new jar I am empty and open.
Like white water are you who fill the cup of my mouth ...
How have you come to dwell with me,
Compassing me with the four circles of your mystic lightness,
So that I say Glory! Glory! and bow before you
As to a shrine?

In "Prime" (the morning prayer) Russell's voice moves
Lowell to worship; in "Vespers" (the evening prayer)
Russell herself becomes the object of worship (as well as
of lust):

Last night at sunset,
The foxgloves were like tall altar candles.
Could I have lifted you to the roof of the greenhouse,

my Dear,
I should have understood their burning.

Similar religious-erotic images can be found in the
posthumous *Ballads for Sale*. In "Thorn Piece," for
instance, her beloved is again an object of both reverence
and sexual passion. Russell's dress here is "red as a
Cardinal's cloak. / I kneel at the trace of your feet on the
grass."

In the "Two Speak Together" sequence the
worshipful "Madonna of the Evening Flowers" is
followed by a number of poems that are patent
celebrations of Lowell and Russell's sexual relationship.
Some of these poems, however, suggest that Russell
sometimes withholds herself. In "Wheat-in-the-Ear," for
instance, the speaker declares, "My hands are flames
seeking you, / But you are as remote from me as a bright
pointed planet / Set in the distance of an evening sky."
Another poem in the sequence, "The Artist," chides
Russell, demanding to know, "Why do you subdue
yourself in golds and purples? / Why do you dim yourself
with folded silks?" Lowell fantasizes her nakedness:

How pale you would be, and startling,
How quiet...
You would quiver like a shot-up spray of water,
You would waver, and relapse, and tremble.
And I too should tremble,
Watching.

In "Bullion," Lowell orders her beloved, "Come, You! and open my heart; / That my thoughts torment me no longer, / But glitter in your hair."

As much as those poems suggest some sexual reluctance on Russell's part, there are other poems in the "Two Speak Together" sequence that hint that she amply fulfilled Lowell's erotic desires. The poems repeatedly capture an intimate physicality between Lowell and Russell: "as you lean against me" ("July Midnight"), "as you press against me" ("A Shower"). "Summer Rain," like "A Rainy Night," places the two women in bed together, listening to the rain:

But to me the darkness was red-gold and crocus-coloured
With your brightness,
And the words you whispered to me
Sprang up and flamed—orange torches against the rain.
Torches against the wall of cool, silver rain!

While most of these poems suggest a sexuality and sensuality that is diffused and generalized, the most remarkable erotic poem of "Two Speak Together" can be read through its metaphoric language as an extended description of a sexual act. The title of this poem, "The Weather-Cock Points South," with its slang reference to male genitalia, may have been Lowell's device here for telling the truth "slant." It also hints at a lesbian sexual act, "going *down*" (the slang term for cunnilingus that seems to have come into the language about 1905):[18]

I put your leaves aside,
One by one:
The stiff, broad outer leaves;
The smaller ones,
Pleasant to touch, veined with purple;
The glazed inner leaves.
One by one
I parted you from your leaves,
Until you stood up like a white flower
Swaying slightly in the evening wind.

White flower,
Flower of wax, of jade, of unstreaked agate;
Flower with surfaces of ice,
With shadows faintly crimson.
Where in all the garden is there such a flower?
The stars crowd through like lilac leaves
To look at you.
The low moon brightens you with silver.

The bud is more than the calyx.
There is nothing to equal a white bud,
Of no colour, and of all,
Burnished by moonlight,
Thrust upon by a softly-swinging wind.

The entire person of Russell may be seen to be a flower
in this poem, just as she is represented to be in other
poems, such as "Song for a Viola D'Amore," or the
description here may suggest much more particularly the
genitalia of the beloved. The poem may describe the act
of disrobing the beloved—or it may be seen as graphically
localized in its sexual meaning. But while Lawrence's
graphic sexual passages landed him in trouble with the

censors, Lowell landed on the best-seller list, perhaps because many readers refused to understand her metaphor; yet it is not difficult to see the flower image of "The Weather-Cock Points South" as an evocative and descriptive symbol for female genitalia: the labia major ("broader outer leaves"), the labia minor ("the smaller ones...veined with purple"), public hair ("stiff"), sexual secretions ("glazed inner leaves"), female tumescence ("you stood up like a white flower"), and the clitoris ("the bud"). Phrases in the poem also suggest knowledge of female sexual sensitivity ("the bud is more than the calyx") and the breath of the lover in an oral-genital act ("thrust upon by a softly-swinging wind"). Perhaps many of Lowell's readers thought this was a poem about the soft south wind as it played on the flowers, but its sexual code is hardly difficult to crack. Thus deciphered, the poem is more frankly and joyously sexual than any of the works of Lowell's contemporaries who came under the strictures of the "Watch and Ward Society."

These poems of both frustrated and satiated love in "Two Speak Together" are followed by a series of poems that introduce a note of anxiety. They must have been written when Russell was preparing to leave again on a visit to her daughter, and also while she was gone. They include poems such as "Nerves," "Strain," and "Grotesque," with their nightmare imagery, their fear that Russell will die before she returns, and that Lowell will go —or has already gone—mad. Attempting to comfort herself with memories of Russell, the poet confesses in "A Sprig of Rosemary" (which Shakespeare's Ophelia tells us is the symbol of remembrance) that even though she cannot see her beloved's face, she remembers her hands,

Sewing,
Holding a book,
Resting for a moment on the sill of a window.
My eyes keep always the sight of your hands

The anxiety of separation is finally broken in the poem "Preparation," in which the speaker, awaiting her beloved, goes to a shop to buy smoke-colored glasses. When the shop man comments, "What a world must be yours ... / When it requires to be dimmed by smoked glasses," the speaker responds, "Not a world ... / Certainly not a world." As the next poem in the sequence, "A Decade," makes clear, it is the beloved who is everything to her, and whose bright presence necessitates shaded glasses. While the novelty of their relationship may have worn off through the years, what remains is solid and complete:

When you came, you were like red wine and honey,
And the taste of you burnt my mouth with its sweetness.
Now you are like morning bread,
Smooth and pleasant.
I hardly taste you at all for I know your savour,
But I am completely nourished.

The last two poems of "Two Speak Together" anticipate Lowell's early death. She was by 1919 suffering from various health problems and complications from obesity. In "Penumbra" a shadow falls over the two women's relationship as Lowell envisions the time she will no longer be there. Unmistakably autobiographical details in this poem—including a description of Lowell's home, Sevenels, "the old house which has known me since the beginning," and her intention to leave that house to Russell upon her death—figure prominently and help to confirm the inspiration and source of the poem sequence in the lives of the two women. The final poem of the sequence, "Frimaire," is a melancholy commentary on the inevitability of aging and death even when one has much for which to live. Lowell compares the lovers to two flowers in late autumn, "Blooming last in a yellowing garden." They have survived though many who kept them company have faded. Like the earlier verse in the sequence, "Frimaire" is a poem of anxiety and fear, as the speaker realizes that one or the other of them must soon die. Describing herself as a coward, she hopes she will be first and Russell, the purple flower, will outlive her, being better prepared to survive alone—"very splendid in isolation"—than Lowell is. The poem ends in both despair and affirmation: "Many mornings there cannot be now / For us both. Ah, Dear, I love you!"

EVEN those later biographers who have understood that these poems are autobiographical and that they reflect Lowell's life with Russell have refused to acknowledge that they are lesbian poems, that they picture not only the two women's spiritual relationship but their sexual relationship as well: "Graphic as it appears, there is an air of amorous innocence about [the poems]," C. David Heyman insists, and then goes on to say that these poems are *"too* graphic to be taken at face value," since, if we read them thus, they become "merely a description of lust."[19] But Amy Lowell appears to have seen "lust" as integral to the fullness of her love for Ada Russell. Once, in great anguish, referring to her obesity, Lowell called herself "a walking sideshow."[20] But no one reading her love poems could have that image of her. It was her ability to love, erotically as well as spiritually, and to record that love in her poems, that restored, and continues to restore to Lowell the dignity of which she was robbed by her appearance and by most of her critics.

## NOTES

1.  S. Foster Damon, *Amy Lowell: A Chronicle with Extracts from Her Correspondence* (Boston: Houghton Mifflin, 1935), 35, 43-44, 56, 60, 65.
2.  Margaret Anderson, quoted in Horace Gregory, *Amy Lowell* (New York: Thomas Nelson and Sons, 1958), 128.
3.  Amy Lowell, *The Complete Poetical Works of Amy Lowell*

(Boston: Houghton Mifflin, 1955), 35. All quotations from Lowell's poetry are from this volume.

4. Jean Gould, *Amy: The World of Amy Lowell and the Imagist Movement* (New York: Dodd, Mead, 1975), 123.

5. Elizabeth Shepley Sergeant, *Fire under the Andes* (New York: Knopf, 1927), 30.

6. C. David Heymann, *American Aristocracy: The Lives and Times of James Russell, Amy, and Robert Lowell* (New York: Dodd, Mead, 1980), 209.

7. Gould, *Amy,* 244.

8. Damon, *Amy Lowell: A Chronicle,* 306-307.

9. Ibid, 482-483.

10. Clement Wood, *Amy Lowell* (New York: Harold Vinal, 1926), 13, 173.

11. Hervey Allen, "Amy Lowell as a Poet," *Saturday Review of Literature* 3, no. 28 (1925), 557.

12. Glenn Richard Ruihley, *A Shard of Silence: Selected Poems of Amy Lowell* (New York: Twayne, 1957), xvii.

13. Richard Benvenuto, *Amy Lowell* (Boston: Twayne, 1985), 11.

14. Damon, *Amy Lowell: A Chronicle,* 441. See also Gillian Hanscombe and Virginia L. Smyers, *Writing for their Lives: The Modernist Woman, 1910-1940* (London: The Women's Press, 1997), 70-71.

15. Ruihley, *A Shard of Silence,* 38.

16. Ernest Hemingway, *A Moveable Feast* (New York: Bantam, 1969), 15.

17. Damon, *Amy Lowell: A Chronicle,* 441.

18. "Going Down," in Eric Partridge, *A Dictionary of the*

*Underworld* (London: Routledge and Kegan Paul, 1950), 294.

19. Heymann, *American Aristocracy,* 251.

20. In his introduction to *The Complete Poetical Works of Amy Lowell,* Louis Untermeyer remembers Lowell describing herself in these terms.

# III. Mary Meriam

1

I know my mind, and I've read many books.
Romance, I thought, would always pass me by,
Lovely romance, her fervent, fluttery looks
Not meant for me. I turned away, too shy.
Then I set eyes on Ada. Through the gloom,
The curtains rising, the thunderous applause—
Or was the thunder mine alone?—the room,
So dark before, struck lightning, and the cause
Was Ada's voice and hair and hands and dress
Playing on all my senses like the world
Seen fresh in childhood. I kept my seat, but less
Sure of my place, myself, my past uncurled
And left me fully present with desire
To hold this woman's flames of silver fire.

2

Daydreaming dim-lit corridors backstage,
I use the laughter, clinking, faint perfume
Of memory and fantasy to gauge
The time and distance to her dressing room.
I pass an open door to Beacon Street,
Some rain and wind, some passersby, the night
Mysterious, romantic, soft and sweet,
Then further down the hallway, Ada's light.
What do I have to give her, what can I
Offer by way of introduction? There
Are perfect words. I lost the words. I try
Again. She is alone, her shoulders bare,
And I can barely keep from kissing them,
To say I found you, and how glad I am.

3

Too stunned for now to leave my place, I sit
Surrendering to time. The play will end,
And then, what gesture will the world permit?
The players bow. The house begins to wend
Its way outside. I walk against the flow
Towards Ada and her entourage, uncertain,
And yet resolved to let my feelings show.
She chats and laughs behind the pitch-black curtain.
*Miss Russell, pardon me, may I express*
*My admiration for your work. My name*
*Is Amy Lowell. Here is my address,*
*And may I write to you?* The white-heart flame
Of Ada's eyes upon me stops my speech.
I tremble for the thoughts outside my reach.

4

Whatever weeps is rain. I say these things
Without a sound, without a trace of longing.
Tonight, nowhere to go. We wear the rings
Of etiquette like chains, without belonging.
What can I do to make my gladness plain?
*Miss Lowell, yes, I will accept your letters.*
Something inside me I cannot constrain
For one more minute melts the years of fetters.
This woman, Ada, this my muse, my dear,
I properly invite to visit me,
To live with me, to be my wife, my sphere,
My garden and delight, my reverie.
Ah, Amy, you old lonely ardent soul,
Slow down and let your Ada learn the role.

5

Dear Ada, it's impossible to stay
Calm in my house and carry on as if
You hadn't let me kiss you Saturday.
I need to hear you murmur, catch a whiff
Of you, I need to hold you close again,
Oh Ada, please, I need to visit you
And give you kisses. Tell me where and when.
And there are other things I'd like to do
(Perhaps I shouldn't write them here—
Perhaps I'd like to let my hands uncomb
Your hair, one summer night, one wild and dear
Warm summer night, where you and I, at home,
Let kisses wander everywhere, the rain
Thrumming a song on roof and windowpane).

6

Unsent. Unsaved. My letter burnt to ash.
I pace and fret and shiver in the cold.
Clocks toll. The seasons go. Don't think me rash.
Spend summer in my Englands, new and old.
We'll stroll among the oaks on my estate,
Then visit Ezra Pound and stay in Kent.
But no, the years must roll, and I must wait
And write again, again be discontent,
And pace and fret again. There is a life
That we could spend together. Others do.
Not every Boston woman is a wife.
How lovely it could be for me and you,
Unseparated, living as a pair,
Purple and crimson blooms in open air.

*7*

O moon so close to full this summer night,
Under your gaze we glide across the grass,
The sleeping flower beds and fountain white
Caressed. Aroused by light, the lily glass
Jiggles and spills her fragrance for the two
Of us. We pause along the path, her face
So close that there is nothing I can do
But kiss her eyes and lips and then retrace
My kiss from lips to eyes. O moon, old moon,
I have forgotten you for this tall flower
Swaying in midnight air within my arms.
I have forgotten every lonely hour
And all my mooning for your blue-moon charms
For her and for a gardenful of swoon.

8

You say you're leaving for another tour,
And all the leaves of all my trees at once
Shrivel and fall without you anymore,
While I sit wooden-headed as a dunce.
You say you need to work to make a living,
And all the fountains of my gardens stop
At once their silly playing, taking, giving,
While I wait tearfully for just a drop.
At once I have too little and too much,
An overflow of wealth I cannot spend
With you. I am a beggar for your touch,
And all my branches ache for you and bend
Hard in the wind, my boughs bend high and low,
Waiting for you beneath cold shocks of snow.

9

Looking at you in firelight, the sun
Begins to seem a far-off dream, the dark
Is all about your hair, and you the one
Giving the firewood its flame and spark;
And I, close by you, circle like the earth
Around you, safe and warm inside your clutch
Of gravity, the question of my worth
To you revolving round my schemes to touch;
To touch you deeper, on the second floor,
To climb the staircase to my bed, and there
Untwist the hesitations more and more,
Undressed in holy half-light, wholly bare;
To turn from outer to the deepest space
And kindle kisses in the fireplace.

10

Rather than lose more time, I take a train
To Ada in Chicago. First I meet
With Harriet Monroe—must I explain,
Excuse, and justify? I want her sweet
Existence twined with mine, if she does too.
Now in the dark again, before the play,
I close my eyes, anticipate my view
Of her, and think of words I need to say.
*Why are you here? I don't like being chased.*
Backstage, she scolds me in an empty room.
*What makes you think that I'm so interlaced
With you that I would...oh, my crimson bloom,
My Amy, here's a tissue for your eyes.
I'm glad to see you, you're a good surprise.*

11

You tell me you've been wounded by the rich
Who woo and use you, deaf to how it feels
For anyone outside their cozy niche
To act in threadbare skirts, downtrodden heels,
To tread the boards, performing for her pay.
You tell me to return to Sevenels.
*I tell you I hear more than what you say.*
*I read the narrative your body tells.*
You tell me you will keep your thespian crown
And tour the dusty states of tragedy;
That you cannot afford to be let down,
You have no standing in society;
And you cannot become my muse and wife,
You have a job to do, you have your life.

## 12

We walk along the lake, the wind is strong,
And Ada leans a little on my arm.
We walk, and where we touch a humming song
Arises, and we both can feel its charm.
We watch a sailboat flying on the lake
And suddenly she says she feels set free,
Maybe she was drifting, now she feels awake,
And she would like to settle down with me.
With me! And she would like to earn her keep
As captain of my ship. We will set sail
Tomorrow, cruise the drink and swallow deep,
Homeward, my bonny, follow the frothy gale,
Through buoy lanes, by helm, and swing the boom.
Tonight, however, we will share a room.

13

This dusk a potion.
Drink it.
Then lucent moon begins her sex dance
Up the sky.
Between the long bare limbs
Of trees
Darker than dusk
Her glow
Arrives, slides, lighter, higher.
Quick,
Where is your bed?
I ask by this cove
Where
I wait for you.

14

Isn't the moon enough, and trees at noon,
Swaying in day or night, alive to light,
Enough to satisfy? What makes me write?
I write because the evening flowers strewn
Across the page are singing a little tune
Of pain that no one wants to listen to.
I want to hear what lilies sing to you,
The things azaleas whisper as you prune,
Transcribe each minute, bundle them in thyme,
And let them blossom in a hundred years
For two like us, who listen to the flowers.
Let lily break the tyranny of tears,
And someday be the muse of rose's rhyme,
Then we can call this earthly garden ours.

15

In this one I am kissing you your lips my bliss
your breasts at last your lips your mouth high bliss

how do I know it's you my fantasy my muse
hidden inside my mind where I alone cry bliss

this January night the cold front fled the air
of fairies floods my bed the window cracked sky bliss

you unattainable and distant never distant
you're in my arms the two of us embraced by bliss

I close my eyes to call you to my bed again
bliss passes lips to lips and thighs repeat thigh bliss

and I am kissing you and Amy's kissing you
and all she ever wants is you is kiss sigh bliss.

What too-bright star, what two-bit life, what lark
Spilling its silky spangles in the dark
Without her. Light that never lights the way
Leaves me unraveled, nowhere. I said stay
For strawberries, they last a week or so,
And we could have them every day, but no,
She goes to see her children. I shall bring
Them here, I'll move the world, move everything
To never miss a day or night again.
Return, return! I'll knit the minutemen
Some suits in revolutionary red
With caps and bells and wooden buttons. *Bed!*
They'll cry, *She wants you in her bed tonight!*
One if by land, and two if by sea, the light.

17

You live inside the letters of this line,
Curving beneath my quill's unsteady flow.
I bring you to my lips, a glass of wine.
Drunk on the purple wind, the curtains blow
Suddenly gusts of raindrops on the sill.
I close the window slightly. Lightning shows
Herself and thunder jolts me. Let me fill
This word with only you. Today the crows
Conversed outside the stillness of my room,
The sameness punctuated by their caws.
Tonight the calm is broken by the boom
Wherein I write my thunderstorm of laws.
I swear the air is fresher from the rain,
And you are rain against my windowpane.

Ada, it isn't great dramatic things
That stir me most, but when the robin sings
After the winter's last snowstorm, or when
We murmur to each other, drift, and then
Murmur a little more before we sleep,
Your voice a song I carry with me deep
In unknown places of my dreaming mind,
A sound I long to hear and hope to find
Again, when daylight brings her happiness.
I like that one, yes, wear the yellow dress.
Before we go downstairs, another kiss?
*Amy, it stirs me most to give you this.*
In our most ordinary cherished way,
Two speak together on a Saturday.

19

Amy, I throw my voice across to you,
Wavering thread without a needle's eye,
Here in the dark embroidered bed of night.
You wrap your voice around, the knot is tight.
A picture rises from the cloth of my
Believing you and you believing too
The subtle weaving of the unknown past,
The vivid presence of our voices making
Poems of tones and shapes. I spool your sound
Inside, I gather every thread around,
I listen close, I speak, my voice is shaking.
What can I do to make this music last?
Lost in the lavish language of your lips,
My threads unravel, and my loose tongue trips.

Ada, my lily of the garden bed,
I draw you flashing through dark grass at dusk,
Your skin the flesh of flowers with the musk
Of spring, knowing the heat that lies ahead—
But what I write is merely metaphor:
You never wander naked in the night;
There are no supernatural flames of light,
No fireworks, beyond our bedroom door.
The sweetness of your body is my art,
My gardening is making love to you,
Your nakedness shakes blossoms from my heart,
I hold you like a flower holds the dew.
The stems of longing are my ecstasy,
The bloom is you and how you ravish me.

21

This garden, is it home enough for two?
This paper where I write, is this our place?
No readers understand my lines to you,
Though half my lines are written on my face.
The purple dahlias nodding in their bed,
Heavy with fragrance, satisfied to stay
For all the world to see, have never bled
The way I do for writing in my way.
It makes me want to bloom alone somewhere,
To live inside a floating world with you,
My Lady of the Moon, in lighter air;
Except there's no such place for only two.
The dahlias' heavy nodding heads agree,
This garden is my paper is my bee.

22

The clipped green lawn goes on in shadowed green
Beneath a sky of shadowed silky blue,
While men and women mingle, seen, unseen,
Along the garden paths lit by a few
Flickering lights. They laugh and smoke and flirt,
At ease with love-in-idleness and phlox,
At ease with us, because of how the hurt
That might have been is safely in a box
You locked. I look at you across the room
And try to keep from staring, kissing you,
Or otherwise revealing how the gloom
That might have been is safely missing too.
I understand the gift that you are giving
Simply by being who you are and living.

23

I picture us together in full view,
The cameras flashing on our faces, side
By side; in fact, without the need to hide,
I'm free to turn my eager gaze on you
And hold you there, as you hold me. I need
To be together in one photograph
With you, our faces happy as a laugh,
Serious too, so everyone can read
How I adore you. Would I kiss your cheek
As well? I'd like to. Cheek and chin and neck,
I'll stop at silk, for now. A kiss, a peck,
A light touch just to give the world a peek.
Someday a sister will be reading this;
I only want to help her reminisce.

The public eye cannot corrupt the two
Of us, no matter how they put me down
Or laugh behind our backs or say I'm through.
Look closely. Who's the poet, who's the clown?
Whose name will last, whose poems gain renown?
We'll hold each other and the truth that they
Will never see. We'll think of Sappho's gown,
White and alive with flowers. We'll be gay,
Of course we will, and I will write my way,
Reveal my love between the lines, and laugh.
Brave words, I know, forgetting what they say,
The world that makes me tear myself in half.
For company, we always have our fields
Of lilies, delicate but strong as shields.

25

The silence stays with me. The hours thin.
The dogs dream, I imagine. You, my muse,
Refresh yourself with sleep, the long day's din
Complete, your flowers on their midnight cruise.
I need this scratchy blanket of the dark
To find one star to cling to, need the moth
Around the flame, the desperate, dreary, stark
Expanse to plunge my needle in the cloth,
To make my memory and prescience one.
Only the old clock on the mantelshelf
Reminds me of the moon becoming sun,
The hours disappearing, dear, myself
As well, for well you know, I am not well.
I do not want to go. I hear the knell.

26

There is the lake that I am dying by,
Apart from you. What isn't falling yet
Will fall too soon, apart from you. The sky
Is lowering lead, the trees are stripped and wet,
The wind is ringing in my ears, this grass
Is gasping, trampled, shot, apart from you,
Taking my reason with you. This will pass,
I hear you in my mind, a soothing coo,
Before the bird, too troubled by the air,
Closes its wings. My reach is lost, my mind
Unknown. I am a very sad affair.
It seems my very breath is undermined.
But then I see your spool of sewing thread,
And comforted at last, I lose my dread.

27

You are the moon to me, my muse and lover,
Rising to fill the dark with silver beams.
Slowly you rise above the earth to cover
My sleeping mind with cloaks and clouds of dreams;
And even in the daylight sky, your streams
Of light show through the ruling blue, and give,
Making the world more hopeful than it seems.
Inside my lines, your love and beauty live,
Etched in my books, with nothing to forgive
Or be forgiven for, an ancient light
That lasts forever. You should know, I give
My fortune, house, and heart, to keep you bright
When I am gone. I write these lines for you
To keep you company when you are blue.

*Ah, Dear, I love you!*

Made in the USA
Charleston, SC
19 June 2015